#om Triston

om Ms. Schroeder

Essential Science ✓

All about Gases

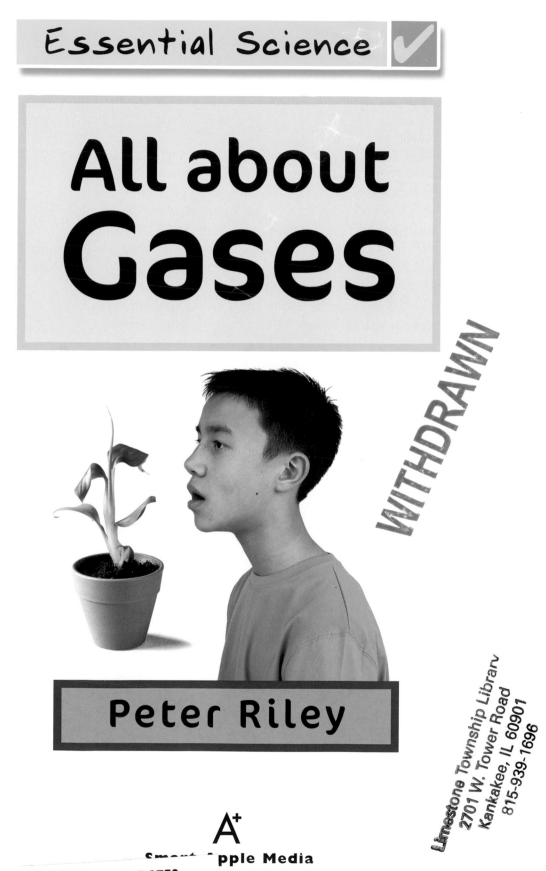

WITHDRAWN

Peter Riley

A⁺

Smart Apple Media

This book has been published in cooperation with Franklin Watts.

Editor: Rachel Tonkin, Designer: Proof Books, Picture researcher: Diana Morris, Illustrations: Ian Thompson

Picture credits:
Sonda Davies/Image Works/Topfoto: 10tr; David M. Dennis/OSF: 13t; Geri Engberg/Image Works/Topfoto: 5; Warren Faidley/Photolibrary: 17; Silvio Fiore/Topfoto: 19t; Christopher Fitzgerald/Image Works/Topfoto: 14; Robert Holmes/Corbis: 4t; KMC International/Photolibrary: 12bl; Doug Lee/Still Pictures: cover br, 16; Moar/Topfoto: 24t; Plainpicture/Photolibrary: 15t; Michael Pole/Corbis: 9; Alan Schein/Corbis: 4b; Paul Seheult/Eye Ubiquitous/Corbis: 7c; Lee Snider/Image Works/Topfoto: 24b; Joe Sohm/Image Works/Topfoto: 22b; Westend61/Alamy: cover cr; David Woods/Corbis: 10bl.

All other images: Andy Crawford

With thanks to our model: Liam Cheung

Published in the United States by Smart Apple Media
2140 Howard Drive West, North Mankato, Minnesota 56003

Library of Congress Cataloging-in-Publication Data

Riley, Peter D.
All about gases / by Peter Riley.
p. cm. — (Essential science)
Includes index.
ISBN-13: 978-1-59920-022-4
1. Gases—Juvenile literature. I. Title.

QC161.2.R55 2007
530.4'3—dc22   2006030984

9 8 7 6 5 4 3 2 1

CONTENTS

ALL ABOUT GASES

These people are surrounded by a mixture of gases: the gases in the air blow on the kites and make them fly.

Gases are all around us. There are many different types, including the gases in the air that we breathe and the gas we cook with. There are also other gases, such as car exhaust fumes.

What gases are in the air?

The gases in the air are oxygen, nitrogen, carbon dioxide, water vapor, helium, neon, argon, krypton, and xenon. Some of these gases are used or made when we breathe.

Can gases be seen?

Most gases do not have a color and cannot be seen. Two gases that are colored are chlorine, which is green, and bromine, which is brown. These gases are poisonous.

Traffic in a busy street makes gases that can be seen and smelled. They can cause air pollution.

Do gases smell?

Some substances release gases that stimulate sensors in our noses. We say that these gases smell. Flowers release gases called scents, which are pleasant smells. When foods go bad—for example, when eggs rot—they release gases that have unpleasant smells.

Flowers produce scent to attract insects. The insects help the plants reproduce by carrying their pollen from flower to flower.

Is a gas like a solid or a liquid?

A solid has a certain size and shape; a gas does not. When you press an aerosol can, such as an air freshener, a gas simply escapes into the air and spreads out. When you pump up a bicycle tire, you squeeze air very strongly to force it in. Liquids flow, and so do gases. The wind is a strong flow of air.

Use the data

When scientists do experiments, they make observations and record them. This information is called data. It may be in the form of a table, bar graph, or line graph. Collect some data about the use of gases in your home by answering questions like these.

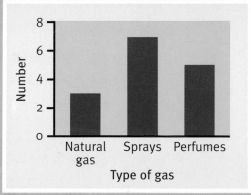

How many things use natural gas? How many aerosol sprays are used? How many perfumes do people use? Make a bar graph like the one shown here. How does your bar graph compare?

You will find data on many pages in this book. Answers to all the questions in this book are on page 31.

THE AIR

The air covers Earth's surface and reaches out into space for 620 miles (1,000 km). You might think that air does not weigh anything, but it does. The weight of the air pushes down on us and is known as air pressure.

Showing that air has weight

You can show that the air has weight by using a simple balance made from two balloons and a coat hanger. When you blow up, or inflate, a balloon, lots of air goes into it. If you tie an inflated balloon to one end of a coat hanger and an uninflated balloon to the other end, you will find that the end with the inflated balloon is pulled down. The weight of the air in the balloon pulls down the coat hanger.

The inflated balloon is heavier than the uninflated balloon.

Where air pressure comes from

You can think of layers of air as being like a pile of soft, fluffy towels in a linen closet. As the towels are piled up, the ones at the bottom are squashed flatter by the weight of the towels above them. In a similar way, the weight of the higher layers of air push down on the lower layers. This push of the air above us is known as air pressure.

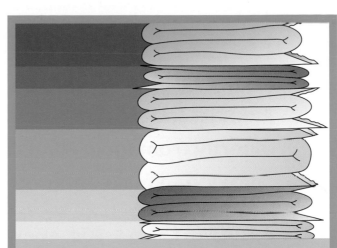

The higher layers of air push down on the lower layers in the same way that towels at the top of the pile push down on the ones below.

The change in air pressure makes the arrow on this barometer move to show how the weather will change.

Air pressure and weather

As air moves over the surface of Earth, its pressure changes. Scientists who study the weather have found that when the air pressure is high, the weather is often calm with clear skies. This makes the weather warm in the summer and cold in the winter. When the air pressure is low, the weather is windy and wet at any time of the year. A barometer measures changes in air pressure and is used to predict the weather.

Predicting the weather

A barometer has a scale measuring air pressure in millibars (mb). It also has words describing the weather, such as rain, fair, and change.

1 What is the air pressure shown by the barometer?

2 What weather do you predict will happen if the pressure falls?

3 What weather do you predict will happen if the pressure rises?

GASES FOR LIVING

Animals and plants need oxygen to get energy from food. Plants also need carbon dioxide to make their own food.

Living things and energy

Living things need energy to survive. They get their energy from food in a process called respiration. This takes place all over their bodies, all of the time. In respiration, the body uses up oxygen and produces carbon dioxide.

Plants need carbon dioxide

Plants not only produce carbon dioxide, they also use it. In daylight, they take in large quantities of carbon dioxide and use it with water from the soil to make food. Some energy from sunlight is collected by the green leaves and stored in the food. The food-making process is called photosynthesis. The food is then used by the plants and animals that eat them.

Plants and oxygen

Plants also make oxygen when they make food. They make more oxygen than they need for respiration and release the excess into the air. This oxygen is then used by animals for respiration.

Oxygen

Carbon dioxide

Gases in water

Gases can dissolve in water. Aquatic animals (animals that live in water) take in oxygen dissolved in the water and give off carbon dioxide, which also dissolves in water. Plants in the water take in the dissolved carbon dioxide to use in photosynthesis and give off oxygen. This oxygen may sometimes be in the form of bubbles, but some of the oxygen eventually leaves the bubbles and dissolves in the water.

When water splashes and forms bubbles, oxygen trapped in the bubbles dissolves in the water. This oxygen can be used by aquatic animals for respiration.

How the gases move around

Plants have tiny holes in the surfaces of their leaves that the gases can pass through. Carbon dioxide passes in and oxygen passes out. Most animals have special organs for taking in oxygen and giving off carbon dioxide as they breathe. Aquatic animals, such as fish, have gills. Animals that live on land, such as humans, have lungs. Oxygen from plants passes into the air or water and then into the lungs or gills of animals. Carbon dioxide from animals passes into the air and then into the leaves of plants. Plants and animals survive by exchanging oxygen and carbon dioxide.

Chemical equations

Scientists use chemical equations to explain how processes work. Here are two equations. Can you fill in the missing words?

Respiration
Oxygen + food → .... + water

Photosynthesis
Carbon dioxide + water → .... + food

USEFUL GASES

Many different gases are used by people every day. A gas can be used to cook your food, make soda pop, and even save your life in a car accident.

Oxygen

Oxygen is an important gas for life, but it also has many other uses. Oxygen makes many things burn when they get hot enough (see page 22). The heat can be used to perform a useful task, such as welding. When a gas called acetylene is burned with oxygen, so much heat is produced that the flame can cut through metal or weld it together.

This flame produced by burning oxygen and acetylene is so hot that it can melt metal.

This crash test dummy shows how the inflated air bag will protect the driver from being hurt.

Nitrogen

Nitrogen is used to inflate the air bags in a car. When a car crashes at more than 19 miles (30 km) per hour, a chemical reaction takes place in the air bags that produces a large amount of nitrogen. The nitrogen instantly fills the air bags and stops the driver and passengers from hitting the inside of the car and badly injuring themselves.

Carbon dioxide

Things will not burn in carbon dioxide. For this reason, it is used in some fire extinguishers. Carbon dioxide is also used in bread making. Yeast in the bread dough feeds on sugar in the flour and produces bubbles of carbon dioxide in the dough. At a soda pop factory, carbon dioxide is dissolved in drinks such as lemonade to make them fizzy. When a can of soda pop is opened, the carbon dioxide escapes into the air, making the drink fizz and bubble.

The bubbles in the bread are made by carbon dioxide.

The bubbles are made by carbon dioxide escaping from the drink when you open the can.

Natural gas

Natural gas formed from the bodies of sea creatures that died millions of years ago. It collected in spaces in rocks. Today, natural gas is extracted and piped into houses, where it is used to heat homes and cook food. If the gas leaks, it can be dangerous because it will burn with oxygen in the air and cause a fire. Natural gas does not have a smell, so smelly gases are added to it so that people can tell if natural gas is leaking.

What makes dough rise

Four lumps of dough were prepared. The table shows what they contained, where they were put, and how much they rose because of carbon dioxide gas being produced.

1 What does the dough need to contain for it to rise?

2 How does warmth or coldness affect how much the dough rises?

3 Predict the result for the empty box in the table. How high do you think the dough will rise?

Dough	Contents	Place	Dough rose inches (mm)
A	flour, sugar, yeast	warm	0.75 (20)
B	flour, sugar	warm	0 (0)
C	flour, sugar, yeast	cold	0.2 (5)
D	flour, sugar	cold	

AIR SPACES

Many substances that we call solids actually have small spaces in them filled with air.

Sponge

The air spaces in a sponge can easily be seen. When a sponge is squeezed, the air spaces get smaller and the air is forced out, even though you cannot see the air moving. If the sponge is placed in water and squeezed, the air can be seen leaving the sponge because it forms bubbles.

The bubbles have formed from air squeezed out of the sponge.

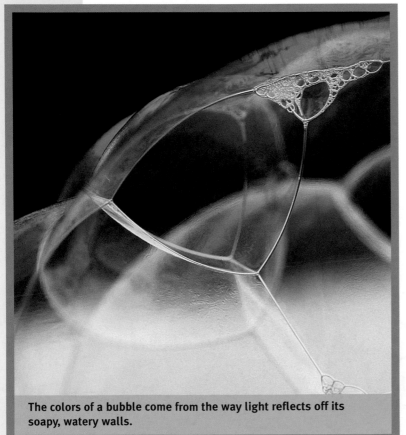

The colors of a bubble come from the way light reflects off its soapy, watery walls.

Soap bubbles

When bubbles rise to the surface of water, they break through the surface and pop. The air in them mixes with the air above the water. If soap is added to the water, the bubble can push the water up until it makes a sphere with thin walls of water. If the soap bubble rises into the air, it can seem to have all of the colors of the rainbow.

Soil

Soil is made from particles that only fit loosely together. This allows air spaces to form between the particles.

As the earthworm moves along its burrow, it takes in oxygen from the air and makes holes in the earth that let the air mix with the soil.

The oxygen in the air is used by tiny living things in the soil and by plant roots.

The amount of air in the soil can be found in the following way. Fill a beaker with soil and a graduated cylinder with water. Write down the amount of water in the graduated cylinder. Then, pour the water slowly from the graduated cylinder onto the soil. When the water appears at the surface of the soil, all of the air spaces have been filled. You can figure out the volume of air in the air spaces in the soil. Look at how much water is left in the graduated cylinder, then subtract this amount from the amount of water that was in the graduated cylinder at the start of the experiment.

Water on soil soon drains into it to fill up the air spaces.

The air in three soils

The table shows the amount of water in graduated cylinders at the start and after testing different soils.

1 What was the volume of the air spaces in soils A, B, and C?
2 Which soil would you expect to have the most tiny living organisms? Which would you expect to have the least?

Soil	Volume at start in^3 (cm^3)	Volume at end in^3 (cm^3)
A	3 (50)	2.4 (39)
B	3 (50)	2.7 (45)
C	3 (50)	2 (32)

EVAPORATION

During a rain shower, puddles form on the ground,
but as the rain stops and the clouds clear, the
puddles gradually shrink and disappear.
This is due to a process called evaporation.

Why puddles shrink

The water at the surface of a puddle evaporates.
In this process, liquid water changes into a gas
called water vapor. Water vapor is colorless,
does not smell, and mixes with the air. When
some of the water has evaporated, there is less
left behind. This makes the puddle smaller.

If there is no more rain, this
puddle will eventually
disappear altogether.

Blowing in the wind

If you hang out wet clothes to dry on a calm day, they dry slowly. This happens because the water that has evaporated from the clothes stays close to their surface. It blocks the way for more water vapor to leave the surface, so the clothes take a long time to dry.

When the air is moving, as on a windy day, the water vapor that has evaporated is blown away, so more water can evaporate from the clothes. This means that windy days are the best days for hanging clothes out to dry.

The wind blows water vapor away from wet clothes.

Three containers of water with different surface areas were left for a day to allow evaporation to take place.

Evaporation and energy

Energy is needed for water to evaporate. On a cloudy day, warmth in the air provides the energy for evaporation to take place. On a sunny day, the heat in the sun's rays provides more energy for evaporation. This means that puddles dry up faster and clothes dry faster outside on a sunny day.

The effect of surface area

The volume of water in three containers (see above) was measured at the start of an experiment and again at the end to see how much the water had evaporated.

Container	Surface area in² (cm²)	First volume in³ (cm³)	Second volume in³ (cm³)
Bowl	62 (400)	61 (1000)	43 (700)
Pitcher	31 (200)	61 (1000)	55 (900)
Bottle	4 (25)	61 (1000)	58 (950)

1 How much water was lost by evaporation in each container?

2 How does the size of the surface area seem to affect the amount of water that evaporates?

GASES ON THE MOVE

Gases can move through one another by diffusion. Heat also creates small volumes of moving air called air currents. Larger volumes of moving air are called winds.

The hot air in the balloon rises above the colder air around it.

Diffusion

If you put an air freshener in a room and close the door, the whole room will smell of the scent when you return. This is due to a process called diffusion. Pleasant-smelling substances in the air freshener evaporate into the air and then slowly mix with it. As they mix, they spread out so that in time the whole room smells pleasant. If there is a natural gas leak, the gas spreads out in the air by diffusion, too, and the unpleasant-smelling gases that have been added mean you can smell the gas.

Air currents

If you put your hand over a warm surface such as an electric heater, you can feel the warm air pushing against your hand. When air gets warm, it becomes lighter than the cooler air around it. This makes it rise. The cooler air takes the place of the rising air and in turn becomes warm. It then rises, too, and is replaced by more of the cooler air. These air currents produce a circling current of air called a convection current.

Breezes

When the sun shines on land and sea, the land warms up faster than the water. The land heats the air above it, and the air rises. Air moves in from the sea to replace the rising air and makes a sea breeze. At night, the water cools down more slowly than the land. The air above the sea rises, and the air above the land moves out over the sea to replace it and makes a land breeze.

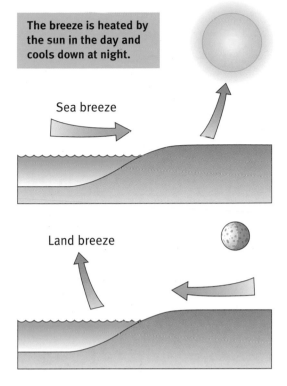

The breeze is heated by the sun in the day and cools down at night.

Sea breeze

Land breeze

Hurricane winds swirl the clouds into a huge disc.

Winds

Winds are stronger than breezes. They form in the same way—by large volumes of cooler air rushing to replace large amounts of rising warmer air. When some oceans become warm, huge amounts of air rise above them and winds then swirl around to replace the air. These winds form a hurricane.

Wind speed

The Beaufort wind scale can be used to estimate wind speed. For one week, write down how the wind feels each day. Use this table to compare each day's wind speed.

Force	Effect	Speed mph (km/h)	Description
0	smoke rises sraight up	0 (0)	calm
1–4	leaves rustle	1–18 (1–29)	moderate winds
5–7	large trees sway	19–38 (30–61)	strong breeze
8–11	difficult to walk	39–74 (62–119)	strong gust
12	severe damage caused	75+ (120+)	hurricane

BOILING AND CONDENSING

When any liquid is heated, it eventually reaches a temperature at which it boils. The liquid quickly turns into a gas by evaporation and mixes with the air. If the temperature of the gas falls, the gas forms a liquid again by condensation.

Bringing to a boil

When a liquid is heated, its temperature rises steadily. Eventually, the temperature stops rising. At this maximum temperature, the liquid is boiling. This temperature is called the boiling point. The boiling point of water is 212 °F (100 °C).

In evaporation (see page 14), water vapor escapes from the surface of a liquid at a temperature below its boiling point. When water boils, the water vapor forms below the liquid's surface and makes bubbles.

Water vapor in the bubbles is lighter than the water around them, so the bubbles rise to the surface.

If you keep heating a boiling liquid, its temperature does not rise any more; the liquid just boils faster. As the liquid boils, its volume decreases because more of it turns into gas. Eventually, all of the liquid will boil away. When this happens, the liquid is said to have boiled dry.

What is steam?

If you watch a kettle boil, you will see white clouds form above its spout. The clouds are called steam, but they are not real steam. The real steam forms just above the boiling water. It is water vapor at 212 °F (100 °C). As the steam rushes out of the spout, its temperature remains at 212 °F (100 °C) and it remains colorless, which means it cannot be seen. When the steam moves away from the spout, its temperature falls because it touches dust particles in the air. The steam changes back, or condenses, into a liquid again and forms a tiny droplet on each dust particle. The huge number of droplets scatter light in all directions, which makes them appear white. The clouds are really condensed water vapor.

The force of steam as it pushes away from boiling water is used to move a steam locomotive.

Water vapor from your breath condenses on a cold mirror.

Breathing out

The linings of your lungs and mouth are moist with water. When you breathe out, some of the water evaporates and leaves your body as water vapor in your breath. On cold days, if the water vapor meets cooler air, it condenses and forms a white cloud.

Reading a graph

A pan of water was heated and its temperature recorded every minute.

1 How long did the water take to reach 140 °F (60 °C)?
2 What was the temperature of the water after four minutes?
3 How long did it take for the water to boil?

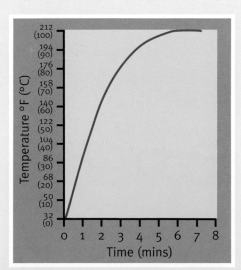

THE WATER CYCLE

Look for a cloud in the sky. In a few days, you could be drinking the water in it.

1. From sea to clouds

A huge amount of water evaporates from the seas every day. It forms water vapor, which mixes with the other gases in the air. The sun's heat warms the air above the seas, and it rises, carrying the water vapor with it. The air cools as it rises, and the water vapor condenses on dust particles in the air to form clouds.

2. From clouds to rain

Clouds are blown along by the wind. When they are blown toward hills, they rise up and cool down. The low temperature at the cloud tops makes the water droplets freeze and form snowflakes. The snowflakes fall through the cloud, melt, and form raindrops.

3. From soil to plant

Some of the rain that falls on soil is taken up by plants. They use some of the water to make food in their leaves, but the rest evaporates inside the leaves and then passes out through the holes in their surfaces. The water vapor mixes with the air gases and may eventually condense to form clouds.

4. Into town and back to the sea

Most rainwater drains into rivers. Some of this water is collected behind dams and forms reservoirs. The water is taken from here to houses, towns, and cities. The rest of the water flows from the rivers back to the sea. This movement of water is the water cycle.

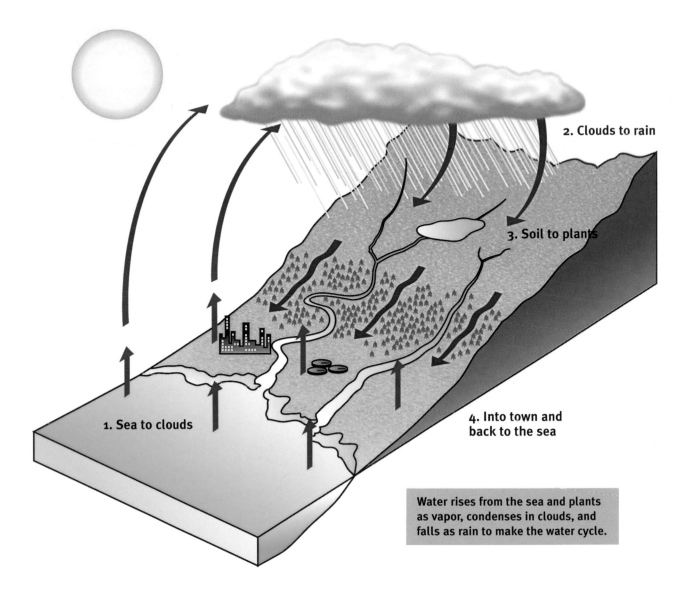

2. Clouds to rain

3. Soil to plants

1. Sea to clouds

4. Into town and back to the sea

Water rises from the sea and plants as vapor, condenses in clouds, and falls as rain to make the water cycle.

How rainfall changes

The bar graph shows the rainfall in a certain place throughout 12 months.

1 How many months had rain?
2 In which month did the most rain fall?
3 How did the rainfall change from March to June?
4 How did the rainfall change from September to December?

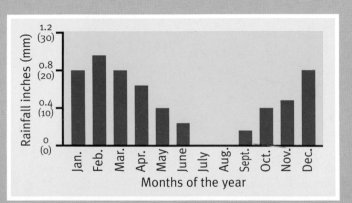

BURNING, RUSTING, AND BUBBLING

Gases can cause things to burn or rust. When some solids and liquids are mixed together, a gas is made. These changes are irreversible.

Air and burning

You can investigate air and burning with a simple experiment. Put a candle on a saucer of water, light the candle, and then place a glass over the top (see picture 1). The glass traps air over the candle. As the candle burns, the volume of air in the glass decreases by about a fifth. Water rises up inside the glass to replace it (see picture 2). The part of the air that is used up is oxygen. Almost all of the rest is made from nitrogen, which does not let things burn in it.

1. The candle uses up the oxygen in the air in the glass.

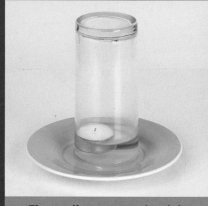

2. The candle goes out when it has used up all of the oxygen. The oxygen has been replaced by water.

Rusting and oxygen

Rust is a reddish-brown substance that forms on the metals iron and steel when a chemical reaction takes place between the metal, oxygen, and moisture. Things made of iron or steel that are left out in the open air rust because the moisture in the air reacts with oxygen and begins to corrode the metal.

Water and oxygen in the air have caused this old tractor to rust.

Bubbling up

When some solids and liquids are mixed together, a chemical reaction takes place and new materials are formed. Sometimes one of the new materials is a gas. It forms bubbles in the liquid that eventually pop and release the gas into the air.

For example, if vinegar and baking soda are mixed, a chemical reaction takes place that produces bubbles of carbon dioxide gas.

Unlike the processes of evaporation and condensation, this kind of change cannot be reversed. It is an irreversible change.

You can make a vinegar volcano by adding a little red food dye to vinegar then pouring the mixture into a bottle containing baking soda.

Burning in different sized jars

A burning candle was covered by three different-sized jars, and the time for the candle to go out was recorded. The experiment was repeated twice. The burning times are shown in columns T1, T2, and T3.

1 What is the total burning time for each jar?
2 What is the average burning time for each jar? (Divide the total by three).
3 Arrange the jars in order of size starting with the largest.

Jar	Burning time (secs)			Total time (secs)	Average (secs)
	T1	T2	T3		
A	30	33	30		
B	15	13	17		
C	25	27	26		

POLLUTING GASES

Some gases are harmful to the environment. Recently, more of these gases have been produced by traffic and factories. People are trying to reduce the amount of these gases being produced.

The wind can be used to turn turbines and generate electricity without producing harmful gases.

Carbon dioxide

When coal, oil, or natural gas is burned in power stations, a large amount of carbon dioxide is produced. Carbon dioxide is called a greenhouse gas. It mixes with the air and makes Earth's atmosphere act like a greenhouse. Heat from the sun passes through Earth's atmosphere, but greenhouse gases stop heat from being reflected from Earth and passing back into space.

As more greenhouse gases build up, more heat is trapped, and temperatures rise. This is known as global warming. It is thought to be causing icecaps to melt and changes in climate in many parts of the world. Because of this, people are trying to find alternative power sources, such as wind, which do not produce carbon dioxide. However, there are many other harmful sources of carbon dioxide, such as burning fuel in cars and airplane engines.

Exhaust gases

When fuel is burned in vehicle engines, harmful gases, such as nitrous oxide and carbon monoxide, are also produced. Nitrous oxide makes acid rain, which damages stone buildings, plants, and fish in rivers. Carbon monoxide is deadly if large amounts are breathed in. Catalytic converters in vehicles remove these harmful gases.

Sulfur dioxide gas from burning coal mixes with nitrous oxide to make acid rain, which damages stonework and kills life in rivers.

CFCs

Ozone is a naturally occurring gas that forms a layer in the atmosphere at a height of about 10 to 20 miles (15–30 km) above Earth's surface. The sun releases rays of ultraviolet light that are harmful to living things. Ozone absorbs most of these rays and protects life on Earth. CFCs are chemicals that contain chlorine and have been used for many years in aerosol sprays and in refrigerators. When these gases are released into the air, the chlorine attacks the ozone layer. This has resulted in holes appearing in the ozone layer that let in harmful rays from the sun. New chemicals that do not contain chlorine are now used in aerosols and refrigerators to help protect the ozone layer.

Aerosols now contain chemicals that do not attack the ozone layer.

Sulfur dioxide pollution

The amount of sulfur dioxide in the air is measured in parts per million (ppm). This means that if the ppm is six, there are six particles of sulfur dioxide in one million particles of air. Here are the amounts of sulfur dioxide in a town measured throughout a week.

1 On which days was the pollution the lowest?
2 How did the pollution level change from Monday to Tuesday?
3 How much did it change from Tuesday to Wednesday?

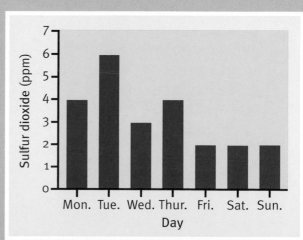

GASES, SOLIDS, AND LIQUIDS

Everything in the universe is made from solids, liquids, or gases. How do solids and liquids compare with gases?

States of matter

Scientists divide all substances into solids, liquids, and gases. They call them the three states of matter. Each state has properties that are different from the other two.

Solids

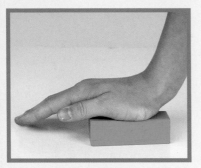

- A solid has a definite shape and volume.
- A solid has mass and weight.
- Tiny fragments of solids, such as grains of sand, can be poured.
- Solids form when liquids freeze.
- Most solids cannot be crushed. However, when a solid, such as a sponge, is squeezed, the air is simply squeezed out. The volume of the actual sponge stays the same.

Liquids

- A liquid has a definite volume.
- Liquids have mass and weight.
- Liquids can flow.
- A liquid takes the shape of the container in which it is placed.
- When liquids freeze, they become solids.
- When liquids evaporate, they become gases.
- When a liquid changes its shape, the volume stays the same.
- You cannot squeeze a liquid.

Gases

- A gas does not have a definite shape or volume.
- Gases have mass and weight.
- Gases can flow and be condensed.
- Gases form when liquids evaporate or boil.

What is matter made from?

It is easy to see what solids and liquids are made from. You can feel the shape and surface of a solid and let a harmless liquid run over your hands. But it is difficult to imagine what gases are made from because you cannot usually see or touch them like you can solids and liquids. Scientists have discovered that all states of matter are made from tiny particles, which are too small to see.

In solids, the particles stick together like bricks in a wall. In liquids, the particles can slide over one another when the liquid is poured. In gases, the particles are free to move around in all directions and can crash into each other and any surfaces around them.

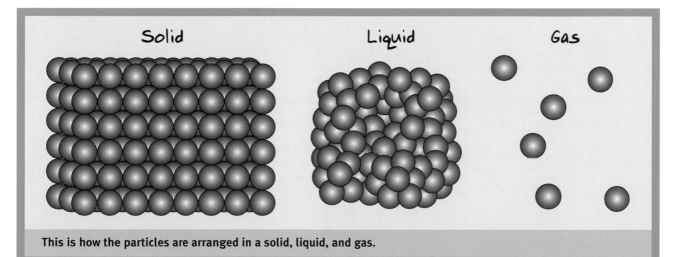

This is how the particles are arranged in a solid, liquid, and gas.

What is the substance?   Which substances are a solid, liquid, or gas?

Substance	Fixed shape	Definite volume	Melts when heated
A	No	Yes	No
B	No	No	No
C	Yes	Yes	Yes
D	No	Yes	No
E	No	No	No

CAN YOU REMEMBER THE ESSENTIALS?

Here are the essential science facts about gases. They are presented in the order you read about them in the book. Spend a couple of minutes learning each set of facts. If you can learn them all, you know all of the essentials about gases.

The air (pages 6–7)
Air has weight.
The push of the air is called air pressure.
Changes in air pressure produce changes in the weather.

Useful gases (pages 10–11)
Oxygen is needed for burning to take place.
Natural gas is burned for heating buildings and for cooking.
Carbon dioxide is used in fire extinguishers, in soda pop, and to make bread spongy.
Nitrogen is used in air bags.

Gases for living (pages 8–9)
Living things need oxygen for respiration.
Carbon dioxide is produced during respiration.
Plants make food in a process called photosynthesis.
Plants use carbon dioxide in photosynthesis.
Plants produce oxygen in photosynthesis.

Air spaces (pages 12–13)
Air spaces are found in sponges.
Bubbles in water are formed by a gas.
Air spaces are found in soil.
The volume of air in the air spaces of soil can be found by measuring the amount of water poured into soil to fill them.

Evaporation (pages 14–15)

When a liquid evaporates, it changes into a gas.
When water evaporates, it changes into a gas called water vapor.
Wind, warmth, and increased surface area speed up evaporation.

Gases on the move (pages 16–17)

Gases can move through one another by a process called diffusion.
Air can flow and make currents and winds.
Air currents are made when part of the air is warmer than the rest.

Boiling and condensing (pages 18–19)

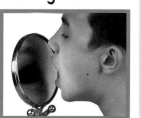

If a liquid is heated, its temperature will rise until it boils.
The temperature at which a liquid boils is called its boiling point.
Heating a boiling liquid makes it boil faster.
Steam is a colorless gas at 212 °F (100 °C).
When a gas cools down, it may condense and change into a liquid.

The water cycle (pages 20–21)

Huge amounts of water evaporate into the air from the sea.
Clouds form when water vapor high in the air condenses.
When clouds cool enough, rain falls from them.
Water returns to the sea and rivers.

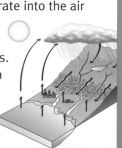

Burning, rusting, and bubbling (pages 22–23)

About a fifth of the air is made from oxygen.
Oxygen is needed for burning to take place.
Oxygen and water are needed for iron to rust.
Gases can be made when some irreversible changes take place between solids and liquids.

Polluting gases (pages 24–25)

Carbon dioxide produces the greenhouse effect in the atmosphere.
Increased carbon dioxide in the atmosphere may be causing global warming.
The ozone layer protects living things from harmful rays.
CFCs have made holes in the ozone layer.
Some gases make acid rain.
Ways are being found to reduce the amounts of harmful gases.

Gases, solids, and liquids (pages 26–27)

Solid, liquid, and gas are the three states of matter.
Gases do not have a definite shape.
Gases do not have a definite volume.
Gases can flow. Gases can be condensed.
Gases have mass and weight.

GLOSSARY

Aerosol can A container that has a large amount of gas squeezed inside it as a liquid. When the top is pressed, the gas sends a spray of liquid out.

Air pressure The push of the air on everything around it.

Atmosphere The mixture of gases that surrounds a planet or moon.

Barometer A device that measures air pressure.

Boiling The process in which a liquid changes into a gas at its boiling point.

Condensation A process in which a gas turns into a liquid when it cools.

Convection currents Currents of air that are involved in the transport of heat.

Dam A huge wall built across a river to stop the flow of water and build up a reservoir behind it.

Diffusion A process in which one substance spreads out in another substance and mixes with it.

Dissolve A process in which a substance separates and spreads out through a liquid and seems to disappear into it.

Dough A mixture of flour, water, and yeast.

Energy Something that allows an object or a living thing to take part in an activity such as moving or giving off light.

Evaporation A process in which a liquid changes into a gas at a temperature below the boiling point of the liquid.

Lungs Organs in many air-breathing animals in which oxygen in the air enters the animal's blood and carbon dioxide in the blood enters the air.

Mass The amount of matter in an object.

Organ A structure in the body that performs a particular task.

Reservoir A place where water is stored to supply buildings such as homes, schools, and factories.

Sensors Ends of nerves that detect changes.

Sewage plants The place where solid and liquid wastes from toilets are made harmless. The liquid can then be released into a river and the solid can be used as fertilizer to grow plants.

Steam The gas form of water at 212 °F (100 °C).

Ultraviolet light Rays of light we cannot see. Large amounts can burn our skin.

Volume The space that is filled by a certain amount of matter.

Water vapor The gas form of water below 212 °F (100 °C).

Welding A process of joining metals together by melting them.

Wind farm A place where electricity is generated by using the wind to turn the blades of windmill-like turbines.

Yeast A substance used to make bread rise and form alcohol in beer and wine.

ANSWERS

The air (pages 6–7)
1 998 mb
2 It will rain.
3 The weather will be fair.

Gases for living (pages 8–9)
Respiration – Carbon dioxide
Photosynthesis – Oxygen

Useful gases (pages 10–11)
1 Flour, sugar, and yeast.
2 Warmth makes the dough rise higher. Coldness makes the dough rise only a little.
3 0 inches (0 mm).

Air spaces (pages 12–13)
1 A = 0.6 in³ (11 cm³); B = 0.3 in³ (5 cm³); C = 1 in³ (18 cm³).
2 C would have most. B would have least.

Evaporation (pages 14–15)
1 Bowl = 18 in³ (300 cm³); pitcher = 6 in³ (100 cm³); bottle = 3 in³ (50 cm³).
2 The larger the surface area, the more water evaporates.

Gases on the move (pages 16–17)
The answer will vary according to circumstances. Some children may give more detailed answers by estimating the wind speed not once a day but at different times of the day.

Boiling and condensing (pages 18–19)
1 2 minutes.
2 194 °F (90 °C).
3 6 minutes.

The water cycle (pages 20–21)
1 10.
2 February.
3 The rainfall decreased.
4 The rainfall increased.

Burning, rusting, and bubbling (pages 22–23)
1 A = 93; B = 45; C = 78
2 A = 31; B = 15; C = 26
3 A, C, B.

Polluting gases (pages 24–25)
1 Friday, Saturday, and Sunday.
2 It went up 2 ppm.
3 It went down 3 ppm.

Gases, solids, and liquids (pages 26–27)
A = liquid; B = gas; C = solid; D = liquid; E = gas.

INDEX